Mortalia and Other Things
by
John Davis

Dedication
To the late Mrs Helen Heward
Who did so much for Madeleine & thus for all our the family

LOLLIPOP MEDIA LTD.
21 DENMARK RD WIMBLEDON
London SW19 4PG

A Book Of Poems
Copyright © John Davis

ISBN 0-9538421-2-6

Published by LOLLIPOP MEDIA LTD.

Designed & Produced by Off The Wall Associates

Printed in Great Britain

An Introduction, By Helen Hackett

This volume of John Davis's poems is at once a record of a life and a meditation on death. John himself cannot fail to have been struck, and probably wryly amused, by how many of the poems grouped themselves together under the heading 'Mortalia'. Many of the other sections too, such as 'O Saisons' and 'Ages and Experiences', are coloured by a profound sense of mutability, of the world turning inexorably, of time slipping away. The evanescent moment is John's theme; and a plangent melancholy is often his poetic tone.

Alongside this concern with mortality runs an iron vein of morality. These are poems of ideas, intensely engaged in reflection and enquiry, manifesting the same ethical sensibility which John brought to bear in his professional life as a paediatrician. Like Keats, he has combined the vocations of physician and poet; but here is no Keatsian retreat into Lethe. We encounter a poetic sensibility as modern as it is Romantic: this poet is a traveller, a witness to many of the tragic scenes of recent history, and a great reader of newspapers. Here is an intellect agitated by public events; ranging from the first moon landing of 1969 to the outbreak of AIDS to the murders of Dr. Harold Shipman. The poems are political in a distinctively personal, humane, undogmatic fashion as their author adopts the potent role of bardic onlooker and commentator: at once of the world, yet not of the world; able to survey the scene with critical detachment but not without sorrow. The public voice of the poems can become a prophetic voice, as in 'Belshazzar's Feast'; and in poems like this, the prognosis for humanity is not hopeful. A mind sensitive not only to the beauties of nature, but to the higher capacities of humankind, finds itself frequently appalled by both the monstrous cruelty and the casual detritus for which our race has been responsible.

In the face of mortality and human culpability, one response might be to turn to God; but these poems find little consolation in that direction. God is not absent from the poems -

indeed, they reveal John as very much a product of his generation in his facility with Biblical as well as literary allusion. However, God enters the poems mainly to be chastised for indifference or berated for cruelty. The religious motif which seems to speak most profoundly here is the crucified Christ, who

> *stares back again with a look*
> *That tells me more than I wanted*
> *To know how he felt on the cross.*
> *('Prague')*.

In one of the most powerful poems in this vein, 'Second Coming - Not so Good Friday', it is pointed out to Christ that he is merely enduring the suffering which God has inflicted on humanity through the ages, with the blasting parting shot: 'Goodbye and will you dare come back again?' What comes to the fore is human conscience. In response to the perplexing questions that arise where science, philosophy, and theology meet, we are urged to resist the allure of simple answers.

All of this sounds grimly serious, yet the poems are also full of jokes. Puns and word-games are relished, as in *'My Old China'*, *'Mr Todd'*, and *'dog'*.

A pleasure in conundrum is shown in *'Why Do I Write?,'* or *'Werde Der Du Bist'*. This ludic turn of thought often produces very good endings to poems, as in *'The Millennium Dome'*:

> *By the blighted riverside*
> *There rose a miracle of rare device*
> *A pleasure dome no one would visit twice.*

Again and again the poems meet one of the essential requirements of poetry, that it should give us lines which lodge themselves in the mind.

John's gift for poetic form finds him aptly dissecting the Thatcherite John Bull in Augustan heroic couplets *('Requiescat')*. This is poem whose ending has had to undergo several revisions as satire on Thatcherism was converted into a salutation to the Blairite dawn, then, in turn, an expression of disillusionment and ant-climax.

Like the 'Queen Mum', also, the poem reminds us that responses to national life are participants in an unfolding narrative; and all these poems, some of which reach back over decades, give us a record of a long life richly lived.

I cannot do justice to John's formal skill without mentioning how grief for Madeleine, surely otherwise unutterable, is turned into a perfect villanelle ('Villanelle'). This piece exemplifies the poetic paradox, known to all ages, that formal rectitude does not deaden but rather intensifies unbearable emotional pain. For those of us who know John, while the poems of engagement in the national conversation give us unmistakably his authentic voice - one of many hospitable pleasures of Davis dinner-table - we must be most deeply moved by the more personal poems. Here is Pip, the beloved dog, and here is the familiar garden pond, converted to a rich inspiration for metaphor ('Pip', 'Depth Psychology').

Each reader will have their own favourites in this collection. My own is 'On the death of the Princess of Wales'. Once again the form is not only beautifully executed, but beautifully chosen: it is the sonnet, the form employed by the Elizabethan Court to celebrate their Queen as a radiant goddess. So many of the qualities of John's poetry come together in this single piece. We find meditation upon a moment which was simultaneously a personal emotional experience and public event, involving a figure known to all. We also find regret, an elegy for the fleeting moment not grasped; and now, of course, in the light of subsequent events, a tender note of elegy for the lost princess.

These are the poems of one who has seen much and thought and felt deeply. 'Speak through me, time', he writes ('Autumn'). Time speaks here, John speaks here, and it is a pleasure and a revelation to sit and listen.

Helen Hackett Reader in English Literature UCL
London, 14th September 2002

Author's Preface

I am not quite sure why late in life I have arranged for publication of this slim book of verse: perhaps it represents a kind of biography, not so much of events as reactions to them, gathered and honed over the years so that something begun in my youth may not have been polished up until old age. I have no idea whether they are any good in a general sense, and I realise that they are unlikely to please those professional critics who notice them at all, but for me they are successful in putting into print what and how I have felt about my passage through the lighted room of the world from entrance to exit and, as such, represent a kind of bid for an admittedly very limited immortality. If they verge on the banal, that is how I am, and at least they are not so obscure as to be a kind of crossword puzzle for who ever may in an idle half hour be curious enough to read some of them. The rest, as was said, is silence: the dead bird left in the road by a passing car, the dead leaves discarded by a deciduous vine.

My sincere thanks to my extra daughter, Helen Hackett, for risking her reputation in writing an overgenerous preface, my niece Anne Williams for publishing a book that won't sell or enhance her enterprise, to my partner Anne - Louise Kinmonth for her encouragement and meticulous proof reading, and to my late sister Ann Szumigalska for critical appraisal. Other acknowledgments are implicit in the contents.

JAD
2003

Mortalia and Other Things

i) O Saisons

ii) Places

iii) Ages and Experiences

iv) Mortalia

v) Mortalia

vi) Bits & Pieces

i) O Saisons

O Saisons

Cuckoo

I think the cuckoo has the saddest voice
Of any bird in spring
Through sunlit woods and shadowed copses calling
While all the rest rejoice
She has no cause to sing
But down a minor third her cadence falling
Mourns the ancestral choice
That took her brood from underneath her wing

Robin

The robin's is the only voice I hear
When autumn brings the fall
From branch to branch in leaf strewn gardens chanting
He follows summer's bier
Beneath its russet pall
And down the scale of middle C descanting
Proclaims the passing year
Reminding us of days now past recall.

Primavera - Spring

Ceres informs the anxious wind
Swallow delineated, searching among daffodils
For scent of spring. Earth under
In the dark below light - seeking bulbs
Dwells her daughter with Pluto
In his silicate palace
There the original waters sleep
Unfamiliar with stars, but sensing
The slow spin of the surface; only
Cosmic rays pierce the filter
That Devonian rocks interpose.
Iron at the heart of it, molten
Gravity squeezing all structure
Out of packed earth and the ponderous sea
Where continents slide on their axles
And the magma surfaces slowly

Life peeps precariously
Between the hot core and the cold
Interstar space not so far
Above absolute zero; in somno aeterne.
Soon our conjunctions
Will wheel away also
Leaving silence for ever
Where once like mice in a cupboard
Our faint voices squeaked
Homer or Newton? who cares?
To know who it was: only Now matters
In eternity's infinite frame
Just a touch of bright pigment
Chiascuro covering the canvas
Of an artist whose name we've forgotten.

Summer

The grasses turn to silver, then to gold
At summer's Midas touch; the days draw in
And birds fall silent; thunder's in the air.
Raffish July; caesura linking hope
With disillusion; dreams to memories;
Precedes imperial August, summer still
But past it's prime, then frail September brings
From the far North a faint sound on the wind
The drums and fifes of the approaching winter.

Autumn

Speak through me time; O let me be your voice
Since you in me, as in all nature work
Your subtle operations; now the day
Fades with the season; and the woods display
Autumn and sunset, coloured in decay.

Autumn has many voices, many acts
Of mourning and of falling: leaves and rain.
Dead leaves that fall, grey rain
That mourns across the stubble, blotting out
The waning glory of September's moon.
Now the harsh tractor tramples down the corn
It's harvest long since gone
Writing with iron pen the delicate wheat of spring
Now on blue uplands the night air is cold
And by the lake the bather pauses
Sensing the water's unexpected chill.

As when a traveller, setting out in spring
Follows a streamlet from its mountain source
Past foothills white with orchards to the plain
Meandering with it all the summer long
Through flowering meadows and slow ripening corn
Until at length he mounts the coastal range
And looking backwards, maps his journey's course
From mountains cloud-confused to where he stands
Watching the wagons bring the harvest home.
I turn my gaze towards the sloping sea
Tossing and turning in its rocky bed
Below the sky on which far distant stars
Prick out a pattern in the firmament
And time and space are one infinity.

November 5th

In the obscurity of a wood
Children are lighting sparklers
One with another in turn.
While they last, one can hear
Shouting and laughter, see
Faces illumined, magnified shadows
Then when all are extinguished
Silence and darkness fall.

Winter

It is all tears now, though we knew laughter once
In those gone days when walking hand in hand
We wandered in the garden of the too brief summer
And never thought to see its ruined flowers
Shedding their petals in the autumn rain

ii) Places

First Visit to Oxford - 1943
Mob Quad

It is late spring: only the interruption
Of clanging bells - to prove the rule of silence
Disturbs the evening air.

Outside the earth is rich with flowers
Fresh daffodils, hyacinth and later rose
Here there's no blossom, nothing that can wither
But stones and shadows and some scholar's ghost.

On these grave lawns time's foot hath gently trod
Here there's no hint of action - only thought
That grows more thoughtful with its own increase
In minds unwearied in their search for God.

Dravidia

Armies depart and leave their dust behind
Now tourists tramp the moghul palaces
Whence Shah Jehan admired his consort's tomb
Black and white marble designate the dead
Pied vultures circle slowly in the sky
The sandy Jumna laps the battlements
And touts and hawkers desecrate the rooms
In which proud ladies drank from delicate cups
Awaiting warriors returning home
With shields or on them - conquerors or slain.

Here in Calcutta other ruins are found
Mansions of merchants sailing from the west
Who came to trade and then by slow degrees
Made themselves masters of the Gangetic plain
Their once well-tended gardens run to seed
The haunt of pariahs and of crows that pick
With ragged children in the detritus
That's left by living - scraps of food or fuel
Mingled with dust and ashes on the path
That runs from past to future, ever on
Into the hazy distance either way -
While glancing upwards one may see far off
The Himalyan peaks that to the north
Mark Asia's boundary from the drifting stone
One fragment - of a broken continent -
That inched its way through the Australian seas
Ere they grew salt or man came on the scene
Cradle of creatures left behind by time
Scorpions and spiders, snakes with eyes of stone
And silent forests of Antarctic beech
That formed coal measures underneath the ice

Where near the pole the twin volcanoes glow
To light the darkness of the six month night.
But who am I, a tiny spark of life
So soon extinguished, yet equipped with brain
And senses able, in its little span,
To gaze upon the whole majestic world
And write these lines as if I were a god
And not a mortal scurrying like an ant
Upon the curving surface of space-time
Till careless Shiva, passing on his way,
Shall crush my body with his dancing feet.

As for my soul: since I have been, I am;
One stitch in that vast tapestry that hangs
Within the chamber of eternity
Made by the Moerae for the Lord of Life:
One spins; another weaves; and then the third
Takes out her scissors and divides the thread.

Africa

The Smoke That Thunders

Like the Thames below Henley
On a warm summer day: rank vegetation
Patrolling dragonflies, a gentle current
Swallows that stoop to kiss the wave-lipped stream
Even an oarsman sculling swiftly by.
Yet over there - upon a distant islet
Elephants are browsing: that floating log
Is eyeing us: it could be dangerous
To trail one's fingers in the water - bilharzia
Infests the water snails - those gnats could be

Malarial mosquitoes, the fly a tsetse.
Out of old Africa always new menace
Nature beating her war drums; nothing's tame
The lion's mane hangs uncombed, the buffalo
Cannot be trifled with; the hunting dogs
Live wild lives of their own. Zebras cannot be harnessed
Nor the leopard stroked; men carry spears
Not rolled umbrellas; their women suckle
Their babies at the breast, are circumcised
To make them faithful to their absent spouse.
The monkeys carry HIV, the dogs get rabies.

If one looks down, to where the surface turns
Ninety degrees into the black abyss
Where the smoke thunders and the rainbows glint
With light refracted in prismatic spray.
Far, far below - where vision cannot carry
The river flows on in a different bed.
Two worlds meet here in a catastrophe
One is quite comfortable; down in the other
Old chaos reigns again - yet we must drift -
No turning back; carried upon the current.
We're over in a moment - not in the immediate term
Foreseen or feared - too sudden and complete
To say goodbye: there is no wieder sehen.

Budapest - 16 June 1989

The crowd is silent, moving slowly past
The coffined bodies where we toss our flowers
A voice intones the catalogue of names
Their age, their occupation and their fate.
There is no chatting but, from time to time,

Singing breaks out to give the heart release
From grief too long contained and put aside.
They sing the anthems which were sung before
On similar occasions down the years
To voice their nation's longing to be free
As were the Magyar horsemen when they ranged
Across the Steppes to where the setting sun
On distant mountains marked their journey's end.

Events recede along time's one-way track
But memories do not fade though locked away
Their first impressions clear as when first etched
By fresh experience on attentive minds.
Since then a generation has grown up
From infancy to early middle-age
Those who were there, already in their prime,
Are ageing now and contemplate their death
Ringing the curtain on completed lives;
These are the names of men who died still young
Exchanging half a life-time for the right
To make their moral choices for themselves
Without which mere existence is our end
Stretching our days upon contracting souls
Preoccupied with getting by or on.

The crowd disperses; yet the Heroe's Square
Is not left empty; it is yours to claim,
No longer ghosts escaped from nameless graves
But the proud owners of your place in time
Your names writ large in history's catalogue
Of those who served not just their nation's cause.
It is upon example that we build
God's city in the kingdom of the mind.

Cracow 1989

These days they come with credit cards, not guns
Not to enslave but just to patronise
Yet if one scratches history's surface here
Down a dilapidated boulevard
Grass growing between the tram lines, children playing
A plot of waste land where used cars are dumped
And dog shit decorates the paving stones
Now a museum - nothing much on show
One finds what used to be a synagogue.
No melancholy broods around the site
Just emptiness, where once God's people prayed,
The echoes of their chanting long since damped
But still above the lintel, not erased
Some Hebrew letters, barely legible.

'It's not too far to Oswiecym' we learn
At the tourist desk: perhaps we ought to go:
'It's there the SS Gruppen took the Jews
All on one day; not one returned again'.
And there we found a Golgotha more dire
Than that grim place where Jesus said 'Forgive';
(But these knew very well what they were doing)
Oswiecym, lest you come to share the shame
Best to call Auschwitzi by its Teuton name.

Today it rained - as if it would not do
For the clear sighted sun to shine upon
What we have come to look at; better the sky in tears
To do our weeping for us; past this gate
Making hell concrete; where no poet is needed
To hold imagination by the hand
Where all material aid was left behind
- Suitcases, watches, spectacles, deaf-aids -
Heads shorn, names changed for numbers, prison clothes
Long rows of barrack huts, an incurved fence
Enmeshed with metal thorns; towers introspective
With gorgon eyes that changed to stone within
Those whom they glared at - hoping to escape.

Bad dreams turned inside out; original sin
Made manifest; evil let loose
Exulting in its power, yet oddly mean -
A child indulging in some secret vice
Out of his parent's eyes, killing flies for sport.
How did this come about; what was God doing
To let his children suffer and torment
Unsupervised, no angel looking on.

And you, Herr Höss, the boss of this mad world
Snug in your villa with your wife and kids
Did you not smell the sulphur on your breath
Or feel the forked tail in your nether parts
Or in the mirror see your dreadful face
Or hear the voice of conscience in your ear
Self righteous in evil since you did
What you conceived as duty carried out
According to your orders and your oath.
Better for you, a stone about your neck
Cast in the sea to drown than serving here
A corporal in the regiment of sin.

But let's forget the men who did these things
Flushed like excreta down the sewers of time
And with what tenderness our outraged hearts
Can summon up in each worse hole of hell
Murmur our benedictions for those souls
Who perished in this place. If there's a God
Who in his wisdom let this come to pass
He'll take you to his bosom; but if not
We'll cherish your sad memory, and for your sake
Attempt to lend to others what you lacked
- A helping hand in carrying your cross
Along the dolorous way to dusty death.

Prague

Necromantic city in which
Like conspirators shadows foregather
As at twilight the alchemist sun
Turns the leaden Vltava to gold

Over the tumbled graveyard
- All that is left of the ghetto -
A bat from the ivy-draped elders
Draws arabesques in the dusk

Down a dimly lit alley
Footsteps sound on the cobbles
But the doors are shut against strangers
And the windows stare out with glazed eyes

******

The puppet apostles strut past
As the clock in the market strikes noon
To make its possession unique
They blinded the master who made it

The menacing murmur of bells
Tolls for Protestant, Jesuit, Jew
The magicians were starved in iron cages
When they asked to walk out in the sun

I gaze at a carving of Christ
He stares back again with a look
That tells me more than I wanted
To know how He felt on the cross.

Penthouse - New York

Rock pigeons roost there on the glassy cliffs
That fall sheer to the street; far down below
The traffic surges with a distant roar
A froth of litter washes on the beach
Where little figures hurry to and fro
Or loiter aimlessly on concrete sands
Hoping to build their castles in the air -
- Air that has visited a million lungs
Stale with tobacco, foul with infected breath -
While up above, where sound waves cannot reach
The leagues stretch endlessly towards the stars
That shower their photons through the inky void
With wave lengths reddened by their headlong flight
From where, before the canyon's lowest layer
Was laid down in the fresh primeval seas
Hopeless and lifeless, nil but stone and sky
To keep the restless waters company,
Some titan sowed the universal seed
Flinging its grains where nothing grew before
To build the spiral stair up which we climbed
Ever more complex and elaborate
Until at last it turns upon itself
No longer idiot or blind or mute
But fully conscious of its circumstance
And able at the future end of time
To understand the past while facing back
An oarsman on time's river pulling hard
Towards a goal that he will never see
Coxless and rudderless above the weir.

iii) Ages & Experiences

Five Ages Of Man

When I was a baby
Walking and talking
Was something the toddlers did
I was contented
With eating and sleeping.

When I was a child
Kissing and smooching
Were things that the older ones did
I was contented
With playing and learning.

When I grew up
To get on in the world
Was something the middle-aged did
I was contented
With courting and drinking.

When I was middle-aged
Becoming feeble and sick
Was something the elderly did
I was contented
With getting and spending.

Now I am old myself
To die and be buried
Is something we all must do
I must be contented
With sitting and waiting.

Time

In my grandfather's day
Time was measured by hoofbeats
Trot, canter and gallop
Complex in rhythm.

In my father's day
Time was metered by rail
Deliberate, simple
Clickety clack.

In my day as at present
Time is continuous
The hum of the engine;
The white sound of the tyres.

How will my children travel?
Silent by bicycle?
Or dismounted again
March in time to their graves.

Caving

Out of bed early: into rubber skins
Then down, headfirst, intently wriggling
Through unlit narrow tunnels wet with slime
Carrying about me what explorers need
Food for a day; a flash light and some film.
Switch on; I've reached the haven that I sought
The cold's enough to take one's breath away
Exhausted but triumphant look around;
If there are walls and roof, they can't be seen
But here's a ledge and there a sliding stream
That silently as nightfall takes its course
From entrance on to exit.

Consulting maps I know where I must go
What I must seek, how long I've got to do
What I came here for, when I'll have to leave.
One can't stay put for ever; must move on
And yet it's good to sit here with a light
And eat our rations, then explore the scene
Comparing notes and taking photographs.
Our voices echo from the distant roof;
We see our own reflections in the stream.

Genesis

Clambering up the familiar tree
From gnarled trunk to fractal branches
I reached out for two apples
Dangling from the top-most twig
Which to choose? one green and probably sour
The other invitingly red
I plucked the red one
Bit it open, found the taste bitter
A worm at the core. It was quite a hard climb
Down to the ground again - leaving unpicked
The evergreen fruit out of reach;
The other I threw away.
Just then the farmer appeared
'Get out of my orchard', he shouted.
I ran all the way home
Into the arms of my mother.

Ars Longa

Like a new fallen leaf she skips down the road
Self propelled by her singing
They tell us that movement is life
But the tree that released her though static
Will put on new leaves in the spring
When she will have withered away.

Adolescence

Searching for windflowers
I got lost in the woods
Brambles barring the tracks.
High in the branches
Doves scolded
And the warbler's song
Shimmered like sunlight
In the new fledged leaf buds
Where the grey wind prowled
Scattering the cloud flock
Over the open sky.

At length I came to a glade
Where last year's shed leaves
Lay undisturbed and a spring
Quietly burbled away
In a moss-lined hollow
The place where the windflowers once
Grew in profusion a delicate blush
On their bridal white petals
Flower heads modestly bowed
Prostrate leaves in the mould
But none are there now; instead
Glossy, erect
The cuckoo pint stands
And a sinister orchid.

Smoking

Why do they do it
Loafing by lamp posts
Passing round packets
Blowing rings in the air.

Despite all we tell them
- Bad for health - antisocial
They rise at the bait
Of the adman's sly slogans.
It is youth's joie de vivre
With no room to dance in
That goes up in smoke.

Picnic - Out Of Eden

Finding a likely place, we spread the cloth;
No cutlery required; and share the feast
A bottle of white wine to slake our thirst
Slices of bread and butter; eggs hard boiled
And for dessert to each an orange pippin
And half a bar of chocolate. Now replete
It being too soon to swim, we fall asleep
Bucolic dreams take over; when we wake
The sun's gone in, the lake looks uninviting
Our litter spoils the sward; we see a notice
Unread before, that warns us not to trespass
(That's why perhaps we find ourselves alone).

It starts to rain; we feel the first sad drops
In disillusion fall upon our foreheads
It's time to pack it in and make for home.

Canto D'amore

I love a lady whose grey eyes
Are clear as winter's frosty skies
And in her spirit pure and rare
As is the glittering upper air
Yet her demeanour's warm and kind
Like to the gentle summer wind.

But should she in her mirror glance
She'd know that nothing could enhance
Her natural beauty; no cosmetics
Improve on nature's own aesthetics.
Nor should his creatures try to edit
Work for which God can take the credit

She would without a blemish be
Did she not err in loving me.

My Old China

Like a chipped cup
In a cheap cafeteria
She stands in the street
Whereas my great aunt's Crown Derby
Secure in its cabinet
Has not as far as I know
Been taken out for a drink.

The End of an Affaire

I have forgot the contour of her face
And cannot recollect what clothes she wore
All she possessed of beauty, wit and grace
To me are as a dream and nothing more

We've had the last performance of love's play
The stage is empty and the curtains close
Actor and audience both, we file away
Henceforth material for the critic's prose

Her image fades: I cannot now recall
The scent and murmur of those happy hours
There is no gate in memories' garden wall
We cannot enter nor revive picked flowers

It's over then; few vestiges remain
Of all we did and said and felt together
Desire, frustration, ecstasy and pain
Have no more consequence than last year's weather

And yet, though memories of memories fade
And what is past can be replayed no more
Time cannot unmake what has once been made
I am no longer who I was before.

Depth Psychology

Part of my property, beyond the house
Below the planted garden, lies a pool.
Beneath its surface, whence the sunlight glances
There's nothing can be seen; but in its depths
Disturbances arise: a fish perhaps
More like the marsh gas given off in summer
By last year's rotted leaves; I am not sure
What residues lie here: we know of lakes
That hide drowned villages, which re-emerge
In times of drought: others where church bells ring
On stormy nights. In my pond only
A rumoured engine - used to remove its bed
To build up an embankment long ago.

To get it dredged would cost a little fortune:
Worth it, perhaps, to open silted springs
And re-establish vegetable life
For fish and fowl to feed on - and, who knows
Somewhere to swim in - free of that dull fear
Which unknown depths engender. Better get it done
Before things go too far and death takes over
The waters that were meant to foster life.

Miss Havisham

Lonely at her window
She watches the world go by.
Everything happens out there
Weather; the seasons; the market
In here nothing moves but the clock
And the spider repairing her web.

Long ago she locked herself in
Refusing the painful involvement
With life in the raw; in here
It's stiflingly cosy; out there
Jostles and jars the world
Getting on like the ant with its business.

Look in the glass once fair lady
Was it so that you looked long ago
When the flowers were out in the garden
And the stars glimmered down from the sky.
Then contentedly humming the bee
Went on her rounds gathering pollen.

One time you sang like a lark
Out of sight in the brightness of dawn
Now the keys of the piano are jammed
And silence settles like snow
Hushing your house not asleep
Just waiting for nothing to happen.

Where did you bury your talents
Deep down in the psyche's dull earth
When will you if ever discover
Roots only can grow in the dark
It's out there in the rain and the thunder
Where bowed not broken the branches
Sway with their leaves in the wind.

iv) Mortalia

Senectus

We've come to the last page
The one whose heading is old age
Let down by what we used to take for granted
- the foundering house by which our ghost is haunted-
In vain to rage; futile to fly or fight
I'm daunted by the dying of the light.

The Dead House
on Zephon Common

Comfort - not much left
Stripped away like paint
Leaving a few shreds
Bare board underneath

If we can be bothered
To apply another coat
There might be a new lease of life
Before having to quit

Better though, unprotected
To brave the harsh elements
Though the wind finds us out
Like a lover's cruel fingers

Letting the hail sting like nettles
Letting the sun blister
Letting the cold clamp
Letting the snow smother

The house of the dead
Slowly disintegrates
Brick by brick; piece by piece
The floorboards give way

Slates have slid off the roof
Doors lurch on their hinges
The curtains blow raggedly
Nothing to muffle the echoes

What's left is only a hint
That someone once lived here
A few fruitless trees; a rectangular ground plan
Filled in with dark grasses.

On Retirement

I've given my last lecture:
No need to prepare another:
And there are no more patients to bother me
I've resigned from remaining committees
There's no point in reading the journals
Nothing I've still got to do
Only some letters to post
Odd jobs to get on with
Like mowing the lawn, washing up.
Why is it then that carefree
I still feel, hanging over me,
The nag of a duty not done
A promise not kept, an engagement
Something not marked in my diary
That I ought to get ready for
If not next week, then sooner or later

Something I'd almost forgotten
When I was busy and harassed.
One more appointment
That I cannot get out of.
Whatever excuses I make.
It would be a relief just to have it
Over and done with for good.
If it brings some peace at the last.

Intimation of Mortality: Angina

I've had all the beginnings that one can
Conception, birth, the primal scream, first smile
Initial steps, first words, first don'ts and dos
First day at school, my first communion
First love affair, first job, first time at war
Of coming under fire, my first born child
My first grey hairs, my very first bereavement
Each a false start; back to the blocks once more
To wait all tense for that releasing bang
To set the world in motion once again
But now it's final and the race is on
For this is the beginning of the end.

After Eighty

We have been sitting for a long time here
Watching the world go by and gossiping
Of this and that, passing the time of day
Transacting business, lounging in the sun
It's getting late now and the party's over:
Some of the company have left; others will
take their leave
When an occasion offers - going home
Or out into the night. We linger over coffee
Till dregs are all that's left and one cold mouthful
That's difficult to swallow, bittersweet.

At breakfast we took tea and scanned the leaves
For what they might predict to shape our dreams
But there's no mystery in dregs; they speak
Of memories only; things long past and done
Forgotten till this moment when we see
The sediment that catalogues our lives
Before they're all washed up. What do I find?
To mitigate the dust upon my tongue?
Some things were good, not always at the time;
Others, enjoyed, yet left a bitter taste
I thank you for the first and blame myself
For what went wrong or did not work out right
No matter; we're together at the end
And grateful for each other's company
We'd better pay the bill and leave a tip
For those who'll have to clear away our things.

Queen Mum

Queen bee or old woman in purple
She got to 100 not out; tame wicket you'll say
But still quite a feat. She remained what monarchs are for
A focus for loyalty, regal embodiment
Of unconscious longings. That's what we needed;
Reassure with a smile while everything else goes to pot
Enjoying her good fortune yet with sympathy
For those with less luck than her own; what's more
She made the best of it; mixing duty with pleasure
Horses and gin, yes, but also parades and charades.
A cheer then for her, upon her millennial birthday.
She saw out two wars, won yet lost
The end of our Empire, the death of her consort
The decay of her family, the end of things as they were.
A daughter of Scotland; descendant
Of Hungarian Saint Margaret and Edmund Ironside the Saxon
Not a German Saxe-Coburg: our first native Queen
Since Mary and Anne. Two cheers then for her
Still waving when it's we who are drowning
In the pink like a baby just born
She'll live on though dead, a grand mummy
In the desert we've made of our hearts
Where sad palm trees sigh in the wind
Three cheers then for her.

On Worthing Beach

Time is running out
Like so many things tend to do
Nescafé, razor blades, cornflakes
Expedients, options, excuses
Season tickets and leases
Money, hope, patience
All ephemeral things
Subject to entropy.

The tide is running out too
Diminished to ripples that shrill
Over wave-warped sands
Lingering in rock pools; leaving
Dead things in its wake
Where once Neptune's horses
Charged bravely up-beach.
Far out on the ocean's bright rim
The salt scream of the gulls
Over the white winged waves
At foot detritus only
Lies stranded on shore
Where dead grasses bend to the breeze
And in an empty shell I hear
Voices of silence.

There's no time for anything much
Just sitting and waiting
Day after day
By the sea-side
For nothing to happen.

Cavalier Treatment

I owned but one horse.
It pulled the plough
Carried me into battle
And in procession at festivals
Once wild of eye, and frisky
Now broken winded and spavined
I got so used to it
I forgot that all creatures
Need a bit of cossetting.
Grow old and tired,
Now it is dead -
A gesture that says it all
And I have no helpmate
To bear life's burdens
Just a hunk of meat
To feed to the dogs.

The End of the Journey

It's been a long journey and those who once
shared my compartment
Have mostly alighted already. Now the diagram shows
That my own stop is imminent; I must look out my ticket
Take down my luggage, pack up my papers
- the unfinished crossword, the absorbing magazine story
That turned out to be part of a serial: I'll never know now
What happened next. Staring out of the window
Watching the landscape wheel past, intermittently dozing
We exchange a few words, banalities only
The others being strangers, walk down the corridor
To eat or excrete, then back to the seat
Which is ours for the journey, pre-booked.
I'm quite comfortable here, don't want to get off
But needs must; what on earth will I find
At the ultimate station; have I been there before
Will anyone meet me; where will I stay
Not much good worrying; you'll know soon enough
Already the engine is slowing, the brakes are beginning to bite
It's pitch dark outside and snow is starting to fall.

Mr Todd

Not quite a friend of the family
Though my father and he in the war
Had a lot of acquaintance in common
And I'm told he was kind to my aunt
When she was suffering from cancer.

No-one quite knows what his job is
A bailiff perhaps or receiver
Putting distraint upon goods
When a final repayment is due
And nothing is left in the bank.

His appearance is not prepossessing
Bald pate, hollow eyes and fixed grin
But he's always soberly dressed
A church-goer, too, we are told
And not a respecter of persons.

He called on a neighbour last week
Quite a party it was - up all night
And the shutters still down in the morning
It seems that he wasn't invited
But would not take NO for an answer.

I met him today in the street
We nodded as if we were friends - though
We've never as far as I know
Been properly introduced.
I want to find out what he's like
But don't fancy closer acquaintance.

v) Mortalia

*On the death of the Princess of Wales; remembering her visit to
Peterhouse to comfort the traduced parents of babies found dead.*

I met her only once - to play the part
Of midwife to a sympathetic gesture
Born of the goodness of her generous heart.
Appropriately gowned in scarlet vesture
I waited on her at the College gate.
It was a pelting day; she came by air
As from the Empyrean: fog had made her late
And dusk was falling: sunset lit her hair.
I glimpsed the muddied cloak before her feet
The flattered queen, the gallant courtier
In my mind's eye but dared not follow suit
In case it should embarrass me or her
Now I regret that as with flowers in frost
A chance not taken was forever lost.

For John Palmer

A month ago we met for tea and talk
You seemed to be your usual cheerful self
Nothing significant was said; we took our leave
Not even bothering to say goodbye
When au revoir seemed more appropriate.
Now everything is past, no future granted
In which to mend or build on what we had
Of mutual understanding or regard.
We did not realise your act was finished
Inconsequential as the mode dictates
And open-ended; needs must, the show goes on
Though your part's written out: no final bow.
- And that is all till time itself is called
And the long run at last comes to its end.

For My Sister,
Anne Szumigalska

At the end there are words
Strung into a sentence
A space in the Times
Nil nisi bonum, thats all.
After that only silence
In the absolute dark
Don't forget me, she pleaded.
We promised; but memory
Needs prompting, as plants
Their ration of water
Else die away
Soon we'll follow her down
To the banks of that river
Whence none may return

We recall our great grandparents
Theirs are forgotten
Their genes, bricolage
To make a new building
Which will founder in turn
Each person a wave
Thrust up, then subsiding
In the infinite ocean
A little sad spray
All that is left of it.
Between sea and sky.

Pip

You disappeared down a hole
Quite a long time ago now
Yet every so often we glimpse you
Or hear your muffled bark
When memories surface.
However it won't be so long
Before death comes to stop up
Even those exits; then two of a kind
Not together, both lost
So deep in time's darkness
That the light of the present
Penetrates there not at all.

Friday 23 December

Pip died - or rather was 'put down', this afternoon. It was clear this morning that it was time for him to go; he could not get to his feet, would not eat or drink and more or less retreated into his shell. Just before the vet came he tried to get up, whimpered a little, passed a stool that stank more of death than shit and was unable to lie down again; finally collapsing on the dining room carpet which before he had never been allowed to lie on. The vet took his paw; Madeleine cradled his head in her arms; the vet's girl whispered sweet nothings in his ear; and without a shudder he fell asleep never to wake again this side of eternity. Thus passed on a good and faithful servant without even a canine vice and the centre of our family - loved by all whatever their relations with each other. It marks the final end of our childrens' childhood and our middle age; coinciding with my retirement and the last of our children leaving home. I have dug his grave with the chimney pot as his headstone in which Ruth last year planted her prize clematis just beyond the greenhouse. I have not met man or beast with a sweeter disposition.

Adjective

(For an acquaintance who threw himself off a skyscraper)

The sentence was your own from first to last
The voice reflexive in the imperative mood
And unconditional. The preposition
Was of your choosing, and no ifs or buts
Could possibly conjoin a different ending.
It leaves us with a question mark unused
Bringing your story to a sudden end
With a full stop. The asterisk that follows
Draws our attention only to a note
To the effect that it was uncompleted.

Christian Morality 1963

I had the fantasy that Christ our Lord
Was present at the trial of Stephen Ward
And Mary Magdalen was also there
(The whore who dried his feet with henna'd hair)
And as with the adultress whom he saved
Albeit that he thought her act depraved
He conjured those who howled for punishment
To look to their own sins - and so relent
But Ward fell bleeding in a shower of stones
Picked from the dirt by Mr Griffith Jones.

On Reading My Uncle's
Last Letter Home - 1916

He did not choose the war he fought
A quarrel of old men
He went because they said he ought
Did not come home again.

He took the long long trail that wound
Up to his calvary
His kitbag spilled upon the ground
Its load of misery

The machine gun's angry stammer
Rapped out it's last commands
The bullets like a hammer
Driving nails into his hands

No matter what the outcome
The minus and the plus
However we complete the sum
He went through hell for us

Oh you who reap what these men sowed
Along the River Somme
What if our poppies showed
The skulls they sprouted from.

Duck And Century

After a party, in an accident
Laughing with friends - brim full of life and hope
It was a tragedy to die so young
The vicar said: she might have known old age
Jilting, bereavement, bodily decay
And death drawn out with no one left to mourn
No need to weep then; since she'd had her innings.

A Stud Groom's Obsequy

A funeral is down to earth
Like making love or giving birth
And so it seemed appropriate
To go and watch two horses mate
Nor was the sad occasion marred
By going from Church to stable yard
What better postscript to a death
Than watching nature catch her breath.

AIDS

With what gay abandon
We tossed our seeds of destruction
On unhallowed ground. Spectres arose;
Cut down they multiplied
Till Thebes, our sin city, was theirs
Sadder than Sodom
Its defences are levelled now
And death has taken it over
No one visits the ruins.

Re-entry Not Permitted

Taken from a king's tomb
And placed in one of their own
Now twice buried, these objects
Could speak from experience of death
If they had voices, not echoes
Echoes that shadow their silence.

Art is our answer to death
For the artist there's no resurrection
But each time his poem is read
Each time his music replayed
Each time exhibited
What he made with his hands out of earth
Clay, metal and pigment reshaped
What ever was mapped in his brain
Lives again.

Caddis Flies

Slender bodies, lace-winged
Fluttering over the stream
They fall in and are carried away
Hardly protesting
'What are they up to?' we ask
'Coupling', we're told
'Don't they do anything else?'
'They haven't the guts', to go on.

A Capital Kind of Punishment

Very early in the morning
Rubbing the dust from his eyes
Themselves too soon to be dust
Waking from sleep to a nightmare
With the taste of death in his mouth
The man who murdered for us
So taking our sin on his shoulders
Unhaunted now by a deed
Finished and done with - quite free
Of evil intentions once acted -
Takes his short trip to the scaffold
Then the long drop down out of time
To hang like a fowl at the butcher's
Goose-fleshed and pallid and cold
Till the doctor pronounces him dead
While the cleric prays for his soul
And the governor nails up his notice.

Was it revenge or deterrence
That led to our taking his life?
Or deep in the psyche, well earthed
Against the sharp shock of exposure
Was it our unfulfilled wish
To kill father or mother or sibling
Buried down there in those days
When will lacked the power to do.
Will we be satisfied now
That our surrogate self has endured
The fate that we feared for ourselves?
Against murder the only deterrent
Is love, as the murderer said
When the judge put on his black cap.

Telly

My world
My only possession
Will vanish from the screen
When I'm switched off.
Other people will go on
Hardly noticing my loss
Till the power fails
And the empty sets
Fade into darkness

I do not know
If my green is yours
Or your red mine
Though the wiring is roughly
Much the same for both
And what the world beams
We receive the same way
Though we choose different programmes

It cannot be true
That when death turns the switch
Things go on as before
Is there another set
In the next room
With a specialist programme
According to taste

Which shall we choose
Music for harp and flute
Played by chaste maidens
Under a famous conductor
Or will we as usual
Opt for violence and sex.

Second Coming;
Not So Good Friday

You claimed that you were God or closest kin
To the all-powerful maker of our world
In which we have to live and earn our bread
And suffer what experience cares to bring.
Should we then sympathise if now we choose
To give you back as bad as what he gave?
He told our fathers not to spare the rod:
This is what scourging feels like to a man.
He made our world a weary pilgrimage
Stony to walk; no rest at any inn:
Now lift our cross and take your own sore steps
To where, all spent, pinned on a bed of pain
You know yourself what part it is we play
In the last bloody act, on stage alone.
'Forgive them Father' - that is what you said;
We do not ask forgiveness, but our turn -
The point once taken - to bestow on you
The pity that he seldom showed for us
Down the dark ages, red in tooth and claw
Black with foreboding, grey with fear and strain,
Through which we travelled to our present pass.
Goodbye; and will you dare come back again?

Nietzschean Calvinism

Those who beg for small mercies
Do not know what they ask:
It involves changing the universe
Re-ordering the geometry of space
And time's arithmetic from start to finish
To weep inexorable fate
From his determined purpose
Even in the fall of a sparrow.
Better put up with it and hope
That what we care about will turn out well
According to the laws that God laid down
In the beginning - for us to discover;
For if it be not so, the cosmos
Is deaf to pleas; therefore best go
Down in defiance to whatever hell
We were consigned to when the first big bang
Set our clocks ticking to the end of time,
No interlude permitted - every part
Assigned and learned by heart to be rehearsed
To an audience of actors.
Do not clap or hiss the players
But boo the playwright if it does not please,
(Who cares not, being long dead).
And yet, perhaps we may extemporise
Making the ending happy if we can.

Lethe

An elusive thought
Slips the mind's grasp
Like a bar of soap
Fallen into the bath
Dissolving away
Till nothing is left
But the Cheshire Cat's grin
A skull in the grave
Which once held a brain.

Todesbett

It was not rape but slow seduction got you
Into his bed: perverse he spilled his seed
Where once our infants sucked; then virus like
Used you to reproduce yet once again
His negative image
But although you now seem half in love with him
And may become forever cold to me
I'll not divorce you nor demand of God
That you should burn for this adultery
But there beyond the yews that ring the church
Where half a lifetime since we made our vows
Not to let dearth, nor sickness, come between,
Couched side by side through that eternal night
Uninterrupted and oblivious
We will not stir till death himself is dead
And love at last returns us to our own.

Villanelle

Winter came early for my Madeleine
Spring brought anxiety, the autumn, dread
She will not see the rose in flower again.

The flowers shed their petals in the rain
The dying foliage changed from green to red
Winter came early for my Madeleine.

The doctors' ministrations were in vain
We knew that by the year's end she'd be dead
She would not see the rose in flower again.

There followed months of breathlessness and pain
The rose had gone; the poppy reigned instead
Winter came early for my Madeleine.

And yet we never heard her once complain.
That she'd enjoyed her life was all she said
She will not see the rose in flower again

It does not seem so long since we were wed
Now it is death, not I, who shares her bed.
Winter came early for my Madeleine
She did not see the rose in flower again.

vi) Bits & Pieces

The Other Apple
(For Dr Harold Shipman)

'Thou shalst not kill; but needst not strive
Officiously to keep alive'

Since men are mortal, why not expedite
The coming dark by turning out the light!
For who's to say this life, so full of pain
Is better than the one we hope to gain
Once we have shuffled off this mortal coil:
So ending all our troubles and our toil.
The stoics thought it better far to die
Than to live on in fear and misery
Or better still to never have been born
Into a life so brief and so forlorn
What better service can the doctor give
Than to make certain that no babies live
Or ease the grip on life of those whose age
Makes it a bore to read another page
Of their long history - so full of woe
When all they ask is to be allowed to go
And if for young and old to die is best
It surely must be medicine for the rest
For being a child is very little fun
And adolescence worse: nor do the run
Of men and women much enjoy the round
Of work and sleep that their horizons bound.
How wise of God to cause a general flood
To drown in sweet oblivion all our brood
How beautiful the world would be, and blest
Were there no men to spoil it for the rest.

Lasciate Ogni Speranza

What the beggars are asking for
Is what we can all take for granted
Food and shelter, that is, and the loving concern of our kin
But to meet their request, we are told
In so many words, neon lighted
Across the thronged platform writ large
Will only encourage them; surely though
That is just what they need us to do
Their hope is just what needs rekindling
When everything else has been lost
Indeed, I'll be damned if I don't
Put a quid in the box just the same.

Haiku

Its beauty faded
Now fragile and delicate
This leaf will soon fall.

The last swallow gone
Like a city besieged
We wait for winter.

To the beat of drums
Time marches past; unnoticed
Life has slipped by.

The wind stirs the leaves
Like a rumour that's whispered
Among the condemned.

Magdalen

They called me harlot since I sold to many
That which my sisters rated at the cost
Of a life's fealty to exclusive love
For just enough to keep me for a day
In my accustomed style of give and take
But let my sisters note that what they trade
At such a price to men and do not give
More in exchange than use of lips or queynt
I would not take except in equal troth
Of heart to heart for ever and a day
And since I have not given my heart away
It still remains as virginal as theirs
And Christ may claim it if some man does not
At his death and at mine forever true
That's why in more than physical embrace
I used my henna'd hair to dry his feet
Which I had washed with my repentant tears.
I have sinned much, t'is true, against the laws
And customs both of men and Gods: yet there's one sin
I never have committed, nor will do
And that's the sin against the Holy Ghost
For proud despair is foreign to my heart
Where humble hope holds sway whate'er my lot
- an all too human being, loose in a world
I did not make or ask for entry to.
But when I take my leave, grown old and grey
I shall expect the only man I loved -
Not physically, with pleasure shared between -
(That I knew not, except to simulate)
But in the heart, to take me for his own
And leave his mother, she a virgin too

For this poor bride who gave him all she had
That was not sold to others for a fee
It's what I live for - and will die for too
When atropos shall snip my tenuous thread
And what I've woven shall become his robe.

Job - Underwriter

Armoured against the universe
In conventional dress and received ideas
We walk securely as Job once did
Unaware that the devil
Has more than one way of peeling an onion
Each making our tears to flow
While adding some spice of life
To what had become a bland diet

Boils and bereavement
The collapse of a syndicate
Into a pile of bad debts
May be just what is needed
To induce us to look to the stars
Instead of our shuffling feet
If we're to find an unstumbling way
Along the dark lane of our destiny.

Moon Landing

*(Written on the night when man first landed on the moon
under a full moon over the Yucatan Jungle)*

I write these verses to the virgin moon
Her destined rape to be accomplished soon
E're man's destructive seed shall find its way
To end her frozen solitude, let's pray
That our presumption will not bring Jove's curse
And earn Promethean punishment or worse.

Man is a cancer growing on the earth
His present greed the cause of future dearth
When, all resources either ruined or spent
Our children's children shall our sins lament
Nature is kind but also cruelly just
She gives her treasures freely to our lust
But should we spurn her bounty once possessed
She'll push the ungrateful baby from her breast.

Like Croesus, man turns all he grasps to gilt
Crying for succour once the milk's been spilt
Henceforward it will be our gruesome fate
To seek for nurture on our empty plate
Nor can we elsewhere try to fix the blame
Since the indictment specifies our name
Mankind ill suits a nature so perverse
We should be called man - cruel or something worse.

With conscience more than other creatures blessed
Why is it man who fouls our common nest?

52

Villers De L'isle d'Adam

With (acknowledgments to Petronius Arbiter)
"Vivre - nos valets le feront pour nous"

Disgust succeeds, our appetite once sated
And gobbled up, the dish seems overrated
Much better to conserve our amorous forces
And spin the banquet out through numerous courses
And what if each of them is only tasted
Our servants will make sure that nothing's wasted.

Political Economist

His was the dominant voice within his field
Bell wether for the flock: he led, they followed
To where t'was best to graze: then chewed the cud
Reducing grass and flowers to elements
Fit for assimilation, grist to mill.
Given a sample of sufficient size
He could predict how members of the herd
Would do and feel and how they would react
To this or that well chosen perturbation
But one important question stays unasked
And therefore never answered in his canon
What makes him wish to comprehend our minds.

It is the devil who understands the crowd
God makes his dwelling in the single soul.

Lady Chatterley

According to D H L
Sex in the head
Is akin to hell
Whereas sex in bed
Is all very well
When it's done and not said.

But if Lawrence was right about it
Why did he write about it
Can it be that the Pen is
Mightier than the Penis?

Catherine At Dogmersfield

From Castile's arid uplands
Across uncertain seas
Then riding a mule
She came to England's dank woods.

One prince died on her; the next
Could not father an heir.
Put aside, a lady in waiting
Climbed into her bed.
Without father or husband she waited
In exile for Christ to possess her
Defending the faith that her Prince
Had betrayed for a handful of flesh
Only a girl then
Hardly menarchial, what did she hope for?
Or was premonition more powerful?
Star crossed with a hybrid rose
Longing for castles in Spain.

Belshazzar's Feast

Pylons grip the earth with metal fingers
Motorways cut across the countryside
Eleven million elms have died
Machine-made noises jarr the tranquil day
And the night's composure is broken
All the strong arms have passed away

Smoke stacks smear the clouds with grimy fingers
And sonic booms percuss the unquiet skies
Where the lark no longer flies
Machine-made noises jarr the tranquil day
And the night's composure is broken
All of the listening ears have passed away

Drainpipes stain the sea with filthy fingers
- Huge slicks of oil begrime the sand-scoured shore -
And dolphins frolic in the waves no more
Machine-made noises jarr the tranquil day
And the night's composure is broken
All of the seeing eyes have passed away

God writes upon the wall with moving finger
Our plates are loaded and our glasses filled
When suddenly the chattering is stilled
Now no unnatural sound disturbs the day
The silence of the night remains unbroken
All of the human race has passed away.

Relativity

Like a dripping tap
Time drops from the future
To collect in the past.
Each tick of the clock
A moment completed
We can't make it run any faster
Or in panic put on the brakes
Whatever Faust may have pleaded
Or Marvell have urged; imperturbably
It goes on in its way, not altering
Speed or direction unless
Love or hate puts its foot down
Or perhaps it is seamless
Flowing past like a stream
Sometimes swift in the shallows
Then deep and slow
Yet the same amount passes
Whatever the rate
As we trail in the current.
Is time out there?
Is it the landscape
That wheels past as we gaze
Out of our railway carriage
Carried from where we got on
To where we have to get off
Others coming and going
At thee occasional halts.

Little Hen Sparrows

Common little byrds
Neat but not gaudy
They spill on the pavements
Like a handful of pennies
Clinking in concert
In and out of the underground
In city and suburb
Picking a living
On the crusts that the rich
Let drop from their tables.
Funny that Venus
Should include in her train
Such drab little creatures
Odd of God also
To note when they fall
Or accept their small bodies
Attached to such feather-heads
As appropriate offerings
At the bar of his temple.

Why Do I Write?

Why do I write this?
Is it for others to mirror
Back to me what it is that I am?
Or for myself in the future
To learn what I was as I am
And thus how I came to be what
I will, if I live, be by then.

The Wisdom Of The East

Visiting a Buddhist bird sanctuary
During an eclipse of the sun
A monk shoved my head down
As I climbed the rope ladder
In case I should blind myself.
But the Hindu who brought me there
Told me to look up to the canopy
Where the storks according to him
Were attaining their sexual fulfilment

When The Wind Blows

Up on the hill tops
Trees rock
To the white sound of the wind

Whence it cometh
Whither it goeth
Are childish enquiries
Implying a purpose
In what is chaotic

Out there over the ocean
Where cyclones begin their dance
Whirling over the wave tops
The waters roll
To the white sound of the wind.

Werde Der Du Bist

Certainly I have become what I am
But is it what I was or I will be?
Yesterday I was the same but different
Lacking the accretion of twenty four hours
And what was needed to adjust to it
Today's stability is but ephemeral:
One spin of the globe, a day's arc
In the elliptic orbit
Alters everything's focus; so does one beat
Of a butterfly's delicate wing.
If when our eyes meet I speak
It could launch something out of control
Into the deep of time where we float
Bobbing on eternity's surface; if I say nothing
It is just as portentous - but how can I choose
Between doldrum and hurricane?
In us two worlds may collide
Or merely approach and go off
On their separate ways in the void
Such near encounters are seldom events
Occur they never so often.

After Sappho

The moon is well past her mid cycle
The Pleiad have dropped down the sky
The night is now more than half over
And the time of our tryst has ticked by
Still hoping but near disappointment
By idself my poor ego doth lie.

Fish

In the green dimth
Sun glassed with water
Slide their elusive shapes
Dark backed and bright bellied
Matching surface and bed

Turning in panic they show
Flashes of darkness or light
To the watchers above
Gazing down on the water.
Or seen from where predators lurk
In the shadowy weed beds
And supine drowned men
Look blindly up to the light.

Such lives are mysterious
Beyond comprehension
By those of us out in the sun
Breathing undissolved air -
Yet our five grasping fingers
Derive from pentagonal fins.

The Millennium Dome

(With acknowledgments to Samuel Taylor Coleridge)

On Greenwich reach did Heseltine
A stately pleasure dome decree
Where Thames, the grimy river ran
Through mudflats never trod by man
Down to the grey North Sea.

So many a rood of barren ground
With a wire fence was girdled round
Enclosing waste land lined by muddy ditches
Where here and there one sees a stunted tree
And vacant lots as big as football pitches
In keeping with the brown-field scenery.

But Oh that gap between the money granted
And the contractors' rising estimates
What if investors sheer off disenchanted
Or serial ministers of state are haunted
By wrong predictions of the likely gates.

Next from the lottery (no chance eschewed
Of making sure the franchise was renewed)
A mighty increment was sometimes forced
With false hopes feeding unreal expectation
For mammon an appropriate oblation.

Over five years without the haziest notion
Of how the money thus supplied was spent
It leaked away, none knowing where it went
To sink untraced into a fiscal ocean.

The shadow of the dome of pleasure
Floated midway in the tide
At a cost no man could measure
By the blighted riverside
There rose a miracle of rare device
A pleasure dome no one would visit twice.

Dog

Putting God in reverse
We find what we seek
ie, love unconditional.

Faithful unto death
He forgives us our sins
Whatever we do to him
Or do not do for him
But we're the all powerful
He worships us.

Requiescat

Farewell, o muse, the Thatcherite John Bull
His bowels are empty and his stomach full
Blithely he steps towards his garden gate
To catch the train for town that's always late.
Comfortably settled in his first class carriage
He scans the Times for birth or death or marriage
(A timely note to influential friends
Will often earn the writer dividends).
Next he imbibes from the financial pages
The nostrums of our economic sages
Satiety's what motivates the greedy
Hunger's the best incentive for the needy
Big bonuses for those who trade in money
Swarming like ants around a pot of honey*
While those whose work supplies our daily bread
With crumbs, discarded by the rich, are fed
Nodding agreement, he falls off to sleep
(Ponies* are what we count these days, not sheep)

* Bacon - Novum oganum Some are like the ant; some are like the bee
* A pony - slang for £1,000

Until, arriving at his destination
He makes his way across the crowded station
Nor heeds the beggars in the doorways squatting
Unwanted men, like bags of rubbish, rotting
In these enlightened times it's not the fashion
To feel - or even simulate - compassion
Then hails a taxi (walking's not for him
He does his daily work out in a gym).
The journey over, at his office door
He boards a lift up to the fifteenth floor
Where like a vulture circling in the sky
He sweeps the city with rapacious eye
Rich pickings can be got from ailing firms
Who've borrowed money on exacting terms
(Fixed assets, sold, will fetch a pretty penny
Though keeping them employed earns hardly any).
It's time for luncheon in a nearby pub
Or, on occasion, at his London club
(No better way to clinch a doubtful deal
Than treat your client to a slap-up meal).
So the day passes and the moment comes
To do the books and total up the sums
I win: you lose - is how he plays the game
And one in which to cheat's no cause for shame
There is no greater pleasure on this earth
Than getting rich when previously in dearth.*
Time to return; but Bull is in no hurry
To join his cow and calves in rural Surrey
The sun's still shining: why not on the way
A bit of rough and tumble in the hay
For whether it is sex one wants, or food
A bit of what you fancy does you good.
What does it matter if he's rather late

---

* *Dante - Inferno - Nessun maggior dolore che ricordarsi del tempo felice Nella miseria*
No greater pleasure does this life afford than poverty remembered

For sitting down to dinner with his mate
There's nought to do, once he's refilled his belly
But watch a vacuous gameshow on the telly
She's well aware he's something of a sinner
But knows in marrying him she's picked a winner
To father the succeeding generation
(Two sets of selfish genes in combination
Will surely in the struggle for survival
Make them much fitter than their nearest rival).
Now, having done her duty as a wife
She leads a very active social life
And once he's out of sight and out of mind
Is free to do whatever she's inclined.
As for the children: better learn at school
To follow, not example, but the rule;
And so to bed: no dreams disturb their rest
Whatever makes them comfortable is best
Whatever worrying trends the polls convey
It will, they're sure, come right upon the day
But lo the dawn with russet mantle clad*
No more blue skies: the news is very bad
Those large in substance but in spirit small
Can't help but read the writing on the wall
(If only we had stuck by Lady Thatcher
There's no-one in the party who can match her)
Yet for the rest the weather is set 'fair'
The people have elected Tony Blair.
Mais plus ça change: things go on as before
The rich are always with us, like the poor.
Pledges and promises are but a snare
Look on their works, ye lowly, and despair.*

---

*   *William Shakespeare - Russet - a reddish colouration red sky in the morning is the shepherd's warning*
*   *Percy B Shelley - Ozymandias*

Over The Hill

The elderly man was taking his dog for a walk. When he had first got it, he was middle aged and it was a puppy; now, as if they had been playing seven steps, it was older and more decrepit than him. He had parked his car at the top of the lane and lifted the dog with effort but gently out of the boot on to the ground, forelegs first. It immediately began - one could call the perambulation a smellie rather than a walkie - to explore the richly malodorous world created by other dogs brought here by other owners and ignoring the fragrance of wild flowers evolved to attract insects rather than mammals. Having made a contribution to what might literally be called a canine conversation, it set out down the lane, looking back every so often to make sure that its master was following Each progressed as a tripod, the master with his walking stick, the dog on three legs to spare an arthritic hip. Their progress was slowish but steady, down the lane between the flanking hedgerows over which the man - but not the dog - could see the fields stretching away into the distance. The smoke from a vertical chimney, dark against the white cumulus, balanced that from a closer bonfire which stood out light blue from the brown woods behind it. Summer was icumen in but had not quite arrived; the breeze was keen and the trees were not yet in leaf though like antlers in velvet. Reaching the top of the shallow rise, the man sat down on a bench, conveniently placed as a memorial to some predecessor who too had often passed that way; feeling his own pulse for the missed beats that explained his sensation of light headedness. The dog stood panting patiently, also quite grateful for the pause in his exertions but expecting to proceed.

Several times the pair passed other walkers going in the opposite direction; courting couples; families; an occasional jogger; hearty women also exercising their pets; a farmer in a tractor doing the rounds of his demesne. The animal, who had no reason to think that it was a dog rather than a human being, ignored its ilk and passed by like the Levite on the other side of the path, snapping at those who attempted any familiarity; his master greeted fellow men and women and their dogs with formal courtesy but was clearly disinclined to pass the time of day with them: their world was an enclosed one. The dog's was a different universe of uncoloured moving shadows and enticing odours, close to the ground like a child, impelled by almost human emotions but with an intelligence geared to the here and now. They were walking westward, as if pursuing the sun as the world slowly spun out of its ambience. The vapour of the passing day had filtered out the blue end of the spectrum to colour the evening in red and gold. Below them a flock of sheep (which the dog, a collie, had been trained to leave alone) shone silver against the emerald of the grass on which they were quietly feeding except for an occasional bleat. The man halted, as if to admire the view, the dog lay down, knowing that this pause was usually a long one; while far away a plane droned by like a bumble bee on its rounds, a light flashing from its fuselage until it disappeared over the horizon where earth and sky met in a blue haze. Already the valleys were in deep shadow, and high above, in the indigo sky, a scattering of stars were just visible. It was as if the world had hatched from its shell of light into the vastness of the illimitable night. They limped on down the slope into the shadows as the sun set, their shapes silhouetted against the still bright sky until both faded into the darkness of the advancing night. An owl called; the shape of a bat flickered in the remaining light; far away a train hooted as it rumbled along its track towards the faint lights of a distant town; then there was silence.

JAD

April 2003